Classic
Yard
Games

Classic Yard Games

An Instructional Manual for Parents, Teachers and Children

By Garry Powell

A

GARRY POWELL taught at many government primary and secondary schools for 32 years, and has watched three children grow up in his own household. He has written several books and many booklets on physical education and recreational activities. The games in Classic Yard Games are games seen and collected from school grounds and backyards over this period.

A

First published in 2002
Robert Andersen and Associates Pty Ltd
433 Wellington Street
Clifton Hill 3068
Australia

ISBN 0 949133 31 0
Illustrated by Roy Bisson
Typeset by Neil Conning & Associates
Printed by Openbook Print, Adelaide

CONTENTS

INTRODUCTION

For as long as there have been children, there has been play. Children play for the pleasure of it all. Play is a spontaneous activity that is child-driven. The games in this book have been an integral part of such play for generations. These games are distinct from structured practice games that are usually instigated by adults for skill acquisition or educational purposes.

Classic Yard Games is a collection of games that children play for sheer enjoyment. They are games that are played in the schoolyard. They are also played at home after school and on weekends.

There are benefits from playing these games: exercise, fitness, gaining physical skills, body coordination, socialisation, teamwork, independence and ethics. But the main outcome should be enjoyment.

The book is divided into seven sections: Skipping Games, Elastics, Hopscotch, Marbles, Running and Chasing Games, Ball Games and Scoring Games.

The text is written so that the instructions and illustrations can be followed by parents, teachers and children.

The equipment needed is minimal, the space needed is small, and the games are self-operative.

The games can be played by an individual, a pair or a group. So the potential loneliness of the only child is catered for, as are partners, best friends and groups.

For the adult reader there will be fond recall of their own childhood, and a desire to share these experiences with their own children or students. For the child reader, there will be incentive to leave some electronic recreation, and go outside and play some 'old-fashioned' games.

SKIPPING GAMES

IN PAST TIMES, this activity has been called 'skippy', and has basically been the province of girls. In modern times, with the acceptance of skipping as an aerobic activity (it is often called 'jump rope'), both boys and girls have become involved. This chapter contains an explanation of the vocabulary of 'skippy' and the equipment used. The chants and rhymes used are the traditional ones, with words that have been used for many years. There are games for individual skippers, best friends and partners, groups and teams.

Terminology

Rope: The rope that is turned to be jumped.

Turners/Enders: Players on the ends of the rope.

Skippers/Jumpers: Players having turns in the contest.

Front Door/Under the Moon: Running into a turning rope that rises away from the jumper as it hits the ground.

Back Door/Over the Moon: Running into a turning rope that rises towards the jumper as it hits the ground.

Double Dutch: Two ropes being turned inwards in an eggbeater motion.

Salt: Slow turning rope.

Mustard: Medium turning rope.

Pepper: Fast turning rope.

Red Hot Pepper: Very fast turning rope.

Out: When a skipper makes a mistake and has to stand out, miss a turn, or relieve a turner, on the end of a rope.

Call in – Call out: Jumpers are chosen by another player to enter or leave the routine.

Kiss: The touching of two ropes.

Keep the Kettle Boiling/On Time: Skippers lined up to enter the rope, which keeps a steady rhythm. Skippers should never leave the rope empty.

Window: A player calls their own exit ahead of schedule.

Technique

Rope length (single)
The rope should reach up under the arms while it is stood on 'doubled'.

Group rope (for three or more players)
4–5 metres long.

Turning (single)
Arms stay close to sides.

Start with rope behind the feet and swing it over the head from there. A steady rhythm should be kept.

Turning (group)
The rope is turned anti-clockwise by two enders, keeping a good rhythm and keeping the loops higher than the heads of the jumpers.

Jumping
Jumpers keep on the balls of the feet and bounce only about 3 centimetres off the ground.

BOUNCE TYPES:

Plain

With feet together, bounce once on each rope turn.

Rebound

With feet together bounce twice on each turn.

Running

Run on the spot so that alternate feet land each turn.

Crosses

Jump with crossed legs.

Wides

Jump with wide legs.

Individual Skipping

One Hundred

One hundred bounces without a mistake – plain, rebound, running, crosses, wides.

Jump Turn

Turn around while jumping.

Astride Jumps

Alternate bounces between feet together and feet apart.

Heel, Toe

Land on right foot and touch left heel to ground, then right foot plus left toe; then left foot and right heel, left foot and right toe; and so on.

Hopsies

Bounce on one foot.

Swings

Hop on one foot and swing the other freely (either in front or behind).

Doubles

Turn the rope fast enough so that it goes under the feet twice for each jump.

Many of the activities, games, and rhymes listed on the following pages as long rope can also be done individually with a short rope.

Partner Skipping

Side by Side
One jumper turns the rope with the left hand, the other with the right hand. All the individual bounce types can be done side by side.

Mirroring
Skipper turns the rope facing the partner, who matches their skips with their own rope. All the individual bounce types can be done.

Visiting
A 'call in' game. The first skipper turns the rope and jumps. They call out the name of another player to join them in the rope. 'I call in my very best friend, and that is ———, One, two, three!' On 'three', the 'best friend' joins the turner in the rope and is 'visiting'. Various bouncing combinations can be done.

Three or More – Long Rope

It is usual in these games that when a player makes a mistake, they become a turner. This is the penalty for a miss. Players gradually progress to join the end of the line again.

Calling In
One player runs in to a turning rope. On the second jump they call the name of another player. This player runs in to be with the caller for the third jump. After jumping the third jump together, the caller runs out the opposite side, and the friend calls in someone else, and so on.

The Ladder
The player runs in to jump first on one foot then on the other. This creates a stepping motion, like climbing a ladder.

The Clock
In this game the player counts to twelve, turning 90 degrees for each jump.

Follow the Leader
Each player follows the task set by the leader. When a mistake is made the player concerned goes to the end of the line. If the leader misses, the player second in line takes over.

Skipping through School
In turn, each player runs through a turning rope without jumping, while all shout 'kindergarten'. On the second turn each jump once for Grade 1; on the third turn twice for Grade 2, etc., up to Year 12. For university, the players enter the rope through the back door.

Cut the Moon

In turn, each player enters the rope, touches the turner's hand, jumps once, then exits on the same side. Each round increases the number of jumps until the last round of 12 (one for each month), where the player must touch the hand of the other turner before exiting.

Favourites

Each turner secretly chooses their favourite TV star, sportsperson, lolly, food, friend, etc. As each player runs through the rope they shout their guess as to these secrets. When they guess correctly they replace the appropriate turner.

Action Games – Long Rope

Banana Splits

The jumper must land with feet astride the rope on the word 'splits' at the end of the rhyme.

I went to the milkbar to get a banana split.
One banana, two banana, three banana splits!

Keep the Kettle Boiling

This is the simple 'on-time' game where players cannot hesitate or miss a loop. A steady rhythm of turning is maintained to the chant:

No missing a loop
If you do we give a whoop!

Five, Four, Three, Two, One!

This is an 'on-time' elimination game that gets harder with fewer players. On the first round, each player must enter the front door, exit the back door, and run around the 'turner' back to their place, to the chant: 'Five, four, three, two, one!' A hesitation or a miss means elimination. All players attempt this round before the second round is started.

Jump beats are italicised and in bold:

*Five four **three** two **one**.*
*Four three **two** one.*
***Three** two **one**.*
***Two** one*
One** and **one** and **one, etc.

Run Around

This is an 'on-time' elimination game that gets harder with fewer players. Players run in through the front door, jump once, exit the same side, run around the turner and repeat from the other side, and so on.

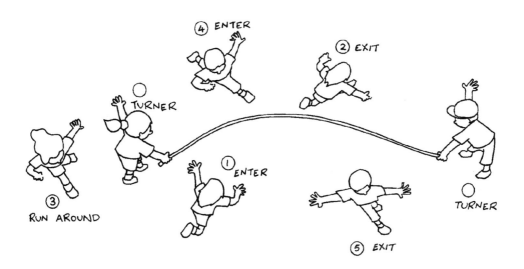

All in Together

All jumpers attempt to enter together. Those that are successful, continue to jump and run out as their birthday month is called. The last player remaining gets 'pepper' for the number of turns equal to their birthday month, e.g. June – 6. The players chant:

> *All in together*
> *This fine weather*
> *A miss is out*
> *And the last gets pepper!*
> *January, February, March*, etc.

Double Dutch

Two long ropes are turned inwards in an eggbeater motion. One rope is held slightly higher than the other. The lower rope is started first, then the higher rope is added. The player jumps these ropes in rapid succession by using a running motion, i.e. one foot at a time.

Double Singles

While turners keep a large rope turning, a player inside the larger rope turns and skips their own small rope. The player 'stands in' to start with both ropes starting together. The exit is forward. This can be made more difficult by a partner entering the ropes and also varying skipping types within the small rope.

Rope Rhymes

These can be used for small or large rope activity sequences; by one to 20 players.

Teddy Bear

Teddy bear, Teddy bear, turn around.
(jumper turns)
Teddy bear, Teddy bear, touch the ground.
(jumper touches the ground)
Teddy bear, Teddy bear go upstairs.
(jumper steps, one foot at a time.)
Teddy bear, Teddy bear say your prayers.
(hands pray)
Teddy bear, Teddy bear turn out the light.
(jumper mimics turning switch off)
Teddy bear, Teddy bear say goodnight.
(jumper leaves the rope)

Birthday

Apples, peaches, pears and plums.
Tell us when your birthday comes.
(jumper chants the months until their birthday,
and then the days until their birthdate)

Doctor, Doctor

Mother, Mother, I am sick.
Call for the doctor, quick, quick, quick.
(turners speed up for 3 loops)
In came the doctor, in came the nurse,
(two more players enter)
In came the lady with the crocodile purse.
(another player enters)
Out went the doctor, out went the nurse,
(both leave)
Out went the lady with the crocodile purse.
(only the original jumper remains)

Johnny, Johnny

Johnny over the ocean,
Johnny over the sea,
Johnny broke the window,
And blamed it onto me.
I told my ma,
My ma told my pa.
Johnny got a spanking.
Ha! Ha! Ha!
How many spanks
Did he get?
One, two, three, etc. (pepper).

Kisses

Down by the river where the green grass grows,
Sat little ——— just as sweet as a rose.
Along came ——— and kissed her on the nose!
How many kisses did she get?
One, two, three, etc. (pepper).

Alphabet

*A, my name is **Abby***
*And my husband's name is **Arthur**.*
*We came from near **Altona***
*We sell **Apples**.*
*B, my name is **Bruce***
*And my wife's name is **Barbara**.*
*We come from near **Ballarat***
*Where we sell **Bicycles**.*
C, my name is ——— (and so on).

Bluebells

Bluebells, cockle shells,
Eevie ivy over;
Mother went to market
To buy some meat;
Baby's in the cradle
Fast asleep.
The old clock says:
One o'clock, two o'clock, etc.

Counting Rhymes

Counting is usually in 'hot pepper'.

Cinderella dressed in yellow.
Went upstairs to kiss her fellow.
How many kisses did she give?

I love coffee, I love tea
How many boys are in love with me?

Lady, Lady at the gate,
Eating cherries from a plate.
How many cherries did she eat?

Teacher, teacher, oh so tired,
How many times were you fired?

Guessing Rhymes

Counting is usually in 'pepper'.

Ipsey, Pipsy tell me true,
Who shall I be married to?
A, B, C, D, etc.

Strawberry, strawberry. Strawberry tart,
Tell me the initials of your sweetheart.

Ice-cream soda and lemonade punch,
Tell me the name of your honeybunch.

(When determined see if he/she loves her/him)
Yes – no – maybe – certainly
Yes – no – maybe – certainly, etc.

Calling in Rhymes

Room to rent, apply within,
When I move out let ——— in.
Calling in, calling out,
I call ——— in and out.
I like coffee, I like tea,
I'd like ——— to jump with me.
Pop, pop, pop,
The boys are calling
For ——— to come in.
——— is the one
Who is going to have fun,
So we don't need ——— (player runs out).

ELASTICS

The basic activity involved in playing elastics is 'jumping'; and as for skipping games, now the jumping in elastics is regarded as healthy activity. The games described can be played by one child (using two chairs as 'enders' to hold the elastic), by two people (one child and the chair as enders), a trio (two enders and a jumper), and by groups (all taking turns). As for skipping games, the words and chants used are traditional.

Rules

- The only piece of equipment needed for this game is a loop of elastic 1–2 centimetres wide and 3–5 metres around.
- The game itself can be played individually, with a partner or with three to eight players.
- The elastic is stretched around the ankles of two people (enders) or around two poles, bins, chairs, etc.
- When a mistake is made, that player is out of the contest and so: replaces an ender, goes to the end of the line or simply sits out the remainder of the game.
- A player is out if they:
  - stand on the band when they shouldn't;
  - fail to stand on the band when they should;
  - break the sequence;
  - miss a step;
  - trip or touch the ground with another body part.

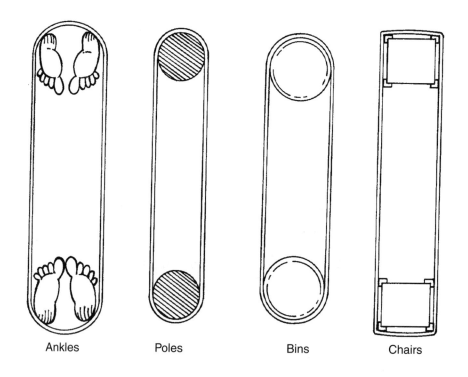

Ankles   Poles   Bins   Chairs

Over the Moon

With the elastics at ankle level the first player uses a stepping motion and passes across the band in a left, right, left, right sequence. Then the player returns to the starting position in reverse order: right, left, right, left.

When all players have attempted this sequence at ankle height, the elastic is raised to behind the knees, then around the thighs, waist, chest, neck, and finally held above the head by the enders' hands.

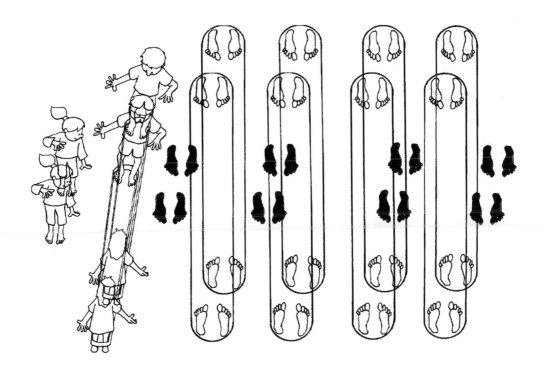

Double the Moon

Jumping two feet at a time (i.e. double-foot leap), the above pattern is done with the elastic at ankle height. Both feet out, left in – right out, right in – left out, both out; then in reverse back to starting position.

Walk the Dog

This is done with a double-foot jump, first at ankle, then knee, thigh, waist and chest height.

Chant:

Right in, right out, right in, right out;
Both in, both out, both in, both on.

OR

England, Ireland, Scotland, Wales
Inside, outside, puppydogs' tails.

What Will I Be?

This game requires a double-foot jump, and involves two moves where the elastic is squeezed between the legs, and two that need 180-degree turns.

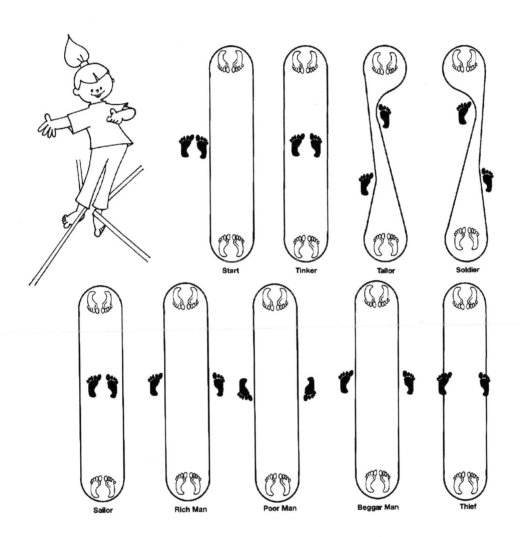

Start   **Tinker**   **Tailor**   **Soldier**

Sailor   **Rich Man**   **Poor Man**   **Beggar Man**   **Thief**

SEQUENCE:

- Feet out, feet in, right foot squeeze,
- Left foot squeeze, feet in, feet out,
- Turn 180 degrees left, turn 180 degrees right, feet on both.
  Increasing the height after each round increases the degree of difficulty.

'W's

The game requires double-foot jumps with feet together, 180-degree turns, catching and carrying the elastic to make 'W' shapes. This is done at ankle, knee, thigh and waist height.

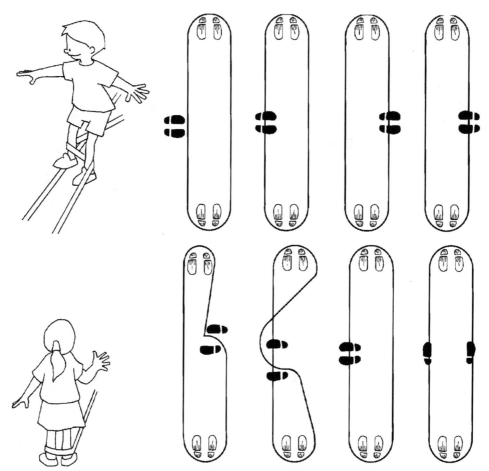

SEQUENCE:

- Feet out, feet on first, feet on second,
- 180-degree turn, right foot under, W,
- feet on first, feet on both.

This is done at ankle, knee, thigh and waist height.

Cross Over

The player stands sideways to the loop, puts one foot into the middle, then touches the ground with this foot and removes it, without the foot touching the elastic.

Then the right foot is placed under the nearer side, picks up this strand and takes it over the opposite side strand so the foot can touch the ground on the far side of this strand. The right foot is then brought to the near side to tap the ground, then back over the far side again – a total, of five far-side taps and five near-side taps all while holding the near side strand on the ankle/instep.

Then the player moves to the other side of the loop where this same sequence is repeated using the left foot.

Double Crosses

This game requires double-foot jumps. The player jumps into the loop with both feet, then out again. This is repeated five times. Then they jump using both feet to carry the near band over the far band and back. This is repeated five times.

Skinnies

This game is a repeat of all the normal activities when the elastic is around two legs or a chair, only this time the band is around only one leg or a thinner pole.

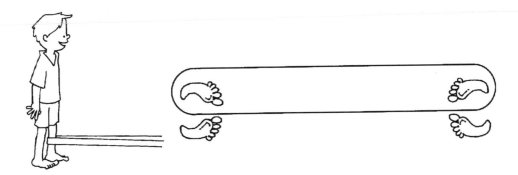

Fats

Instead of the enders standing with feet together, they stand with legs wide apart, or there are two people at each end.

Jogs

This can be done in normal, fats or skinnies elastics. Feet are moved in a jogging motion, one foot at a time. The feet should not be completely still at any time – one foot should always be moving.

EXAMPLE:

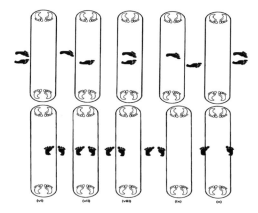

SEQUENCE:

- Feet out, right in, left as well, right out,
- left as well, left in, right as well, left out,
- right as well, both on (9 movements).

Gymnastics

This game involves gymnastics skills to enter or exit the loop, e.g. cartwheel. After entry a normal jump sequence is completed. This is done at ankle, knee, thigh, waist height.

Follow the Leader

Each player follows the task set by the leader. When a mistake is made the player concerned replaces one of the enders. This game can be made as difficult as the skill level of the players. Many patterns can be made by the leader but usually the start is with two feet out, the finish with two feet on, and the total number of jumps is limited to 10 or less.

Partners

Two people join hands and complete the designated sequence at exactly the same time. This is done at ankle, knee, thigh and waist height.

EXAMPLE:

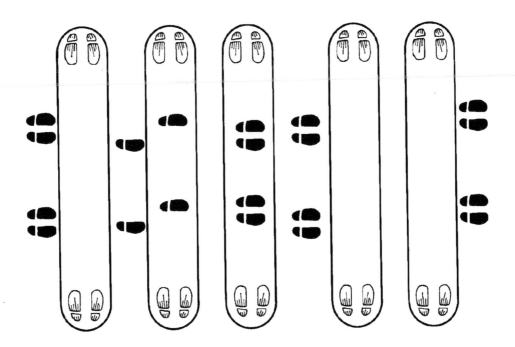

HOPSCOTCH

IT IS POSSIBLE to play hopscotch on any surface, but it is best played on a paved area (for example, asphalt or concrete). In schoolyards, hopscotch courts are often permanently painted on the ground; and in backyards these courts are usually chalked in. All types of this game can be played by individual players (each taking turns), by pairs taking turns in a one-on-one contest, or by groups each taking their turn. The optimum group size is 3–5, and then there is not a huge amount of waiting or 'inactivity time'.

Rules

- A stone or stick is used by each player as their individual marker (taw).
- The aim is to hop and jump through the court in a specific pattern without the feet touching the lines and without putting a hand down to gain balance.
- When a line is landed upon either by a marker or a foot, the player loses their turn.

Classic Hopscotch

The player starts by throwing their taw into box 1. If it stays inside the box they then are allowed to hop the court.

In this classic court the sequence is one foot in boxes 1, 4 and 7; and simultaneous two feet landing in boxes 2/3, 5/6 and REST.

So the count would be: 1 – 2 – 1 – 2 – 1 – 2.

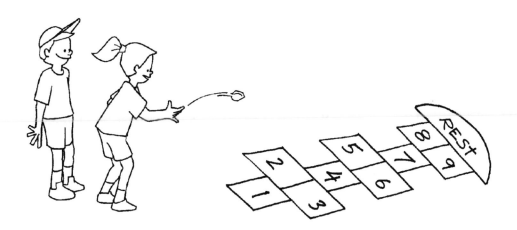

On reaching REST, the player does a 180-degree jump-turn to face back down the court, landing on two feet. They then retrace their steps, picking up their taw from box 1 while standing in 2/3. Then the next player has a turn.

On the next turn the taw must land in box 2 and so on in consecutive turns until they have completed boxes 1–7.

Monopoly

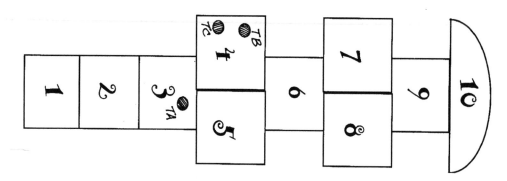

This is similar to Classic Hopscotch, with one major variation. Each player throws their taw in readiness for their next shot before the next player has their turn. The taws are left in the boxes and are out of bounds for other players (monopoly).

In the diagram for monopoly there are three taws pictured. The normal foot pattern would be: 1 – 1 – 1 – 2 – 1 – 2 – 1 – 2 – 2 – 1 – 2 – 1 – 2 – 1 – 1 – 1. But player C cannot set foot in boxes 3 and 4, so their foot pattern would be: 1 – 1 – 1 – 1 – 2 – 1 – 2 – 2 – 1 – 2 – 1 – 1 – 1 – 1.

Court Variations

Classic and monopoly hopscotch can be played on a variety of courts.

The rules are the same for all courts, although the foot pattern changes considerably depending on the court.

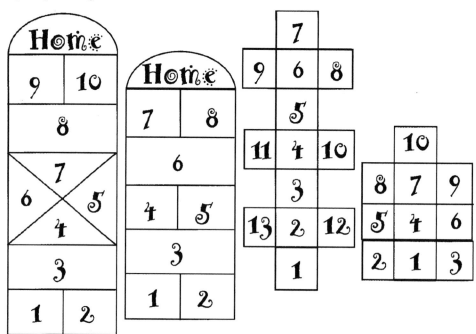

Snail Hopscotch

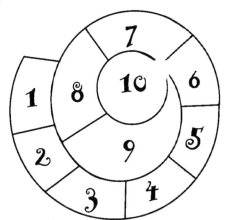

The player starts by throwing their taw into box 1. The progression is all by hopping; and the taw has to be kicked into boxes 2–10 before the player hops along. If either the taw or a foot rests on a line, the player loses a turn.

There are four progressions:

1 Preferred foot: 1–10.
2 Non-preferred foot: 1–10.
3 Preferred foot: 1–10 then 10–1.
4 Non-preferred foot: 1–10 then 10–1.

Physical Variations

The court is hopped through using physical limitations.

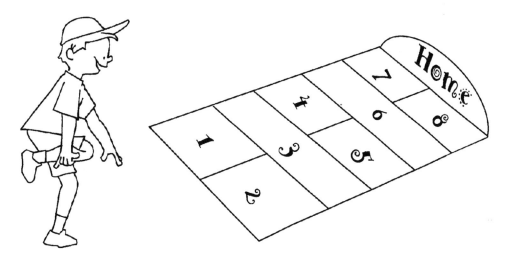

1 With eyes shut – 'blindfolds'.
2 With the taw on the players' head – 'heads'.
3 With the taw balanced on the instep of the non-hopping foot – 'football'.
4 Holding a designated body part – 'hospitals'.

Team Hopscotch

For four or more players.

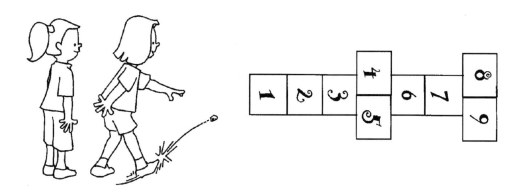

Any of the hopscotch variations can be played in teams.

After an agreed number of turns, the finishing position of each teach member is totalled. The team with the greatest total wins.

Category Hopscotch

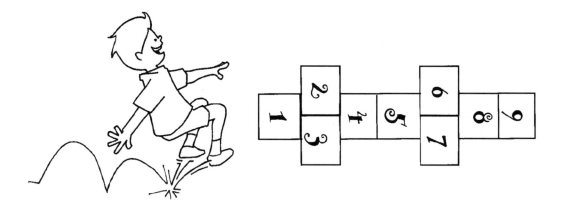

There is no taw used in this game. Players hop on one foot in each box and in even rhythm. As they land in each box they must call out an item in a set category. To stand on a line or to miss a call means to lose a turn.

EXAMPLES:

Girls' names   Pop stars
Boys' names   Colours
Towns   Wild animals
Countries   Birds
Football players   Counting rhymes

Ball Hopscotch

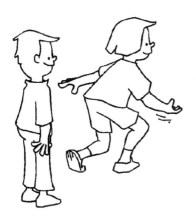
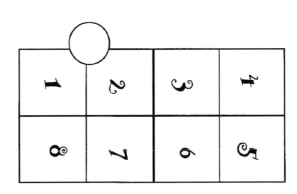

Boxes are approximately 1 metre square.

The player rolls the ball into box 1, hops in after it, picks it up while it is still in box 1 and bounces it. Then they roll the ball into box 2, hop in, pick it up and bounce it, and so on.

As the game progresses, the skill needed increases.

1   Every second box (the slow rolling of the ball is more important).
2   Every third box.
3   Bounce the number of times equal to the box numeral.
4   Throw – clap and catch and so on.

MARBLES

Marbles is a game that is seasonal in popularity. Played by boys only a century ago, it is now popular with both girls and boys. This chapter explains the vocabulary of marbles, the types of equipment, the basic skills of 'firing' a marble, plus the rules and tactics of various games. Marbles can be played on any surface; but the best and most commonly used is a hard packed dirt area.

Skills

Marbles can be played by an individual (taking both turns to shoot), by two people as direct opponents, or by a group of up to 6 people.

Releasing the marble from the hand is called 'firing' or 'shooting'. The firing marble is called the taw. There are two methods of firing: 'basic' and 'advanced'.

Basic Firing

The marble is placed in the crook of the index finger that is formed by curling this finger as a loose fist is formed. The marble rests on the second segment of this finger, which is held slightly apart from the rest of the fist.

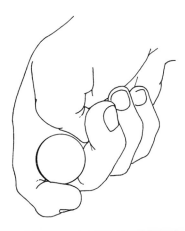

The thumb is placed behind the marble, pressing into the second segment of the index finger. From this ready position the marble is fired by flicking the thumb outwards to propel the marble forward. The power of the flick dictates the speed at which the marble travels and therefore the distance also.

To steady the hand to fire, the knuckles of the second, third and little fingers are placed on the ground. When firing for distance the hand can be placed on the player's knee or hip to gain a higher trajectory. At all times one knuckle must be in contact with the ground, knee or hip.

Advanced Firing

With a loose fist, the marble is placed between the tips of the index and second fingers. The thumb is curled under the marble so that this taw rests on the nail and the top segment. As in the basic skill, the marble is propelled by the thumb pushing forwards in a flicking motion.

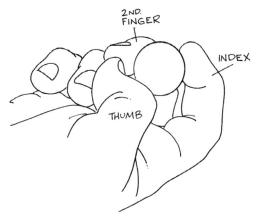

Terminology

Taw: The marble that is fired.
Dibs or ducks: The target marbles.
The ring: The area from which the target marbles have to be hit out by the taws.
The line: The line to which players toss their taws to see who fires first.
For keeps: Each player keeps the target marbles they hit from the ring.

For fun: All target marbles are returned to their owners at the end of the game.
Stick: When the taw stops immediately after hitting a dib.
Slips: When the taw slips from the hand while preparing to fire.
Fudge: When the arm or wrist is used to help propel the marble (not allowed).
Dribble: A soft shot to gain position.
Lag: Another term for a dribble shot.

Types of Marbles

Aggies: Agate or other stone.
Steelies: Ball bearings or pinball balls.
Bloods: Red and white stone.
Tom bowlers: Extra large marbles.
Honey pots: Fawn and orange agate.
Honey reels: Brown and white stone.
Glassies: Clear glass.
Rainbows: Multicoloured.
Milkies: Opaque glass.
Cat's eye: Clear glass with a strip of colour in the middle.
Galaxies: Clear glass with coloured swirls in the middle.

Little Ring

Each player places one marble in a ring of approximately 12 centimetres in diameter.
The starting line is drawn approximately 4–5 metres away.

To determine the order of firing, players throw their marbles from the same place
(e.g. the far side of the ring) to see who gets closest to the line.

The aim of the game is to hit the dib marbles out of the ring.

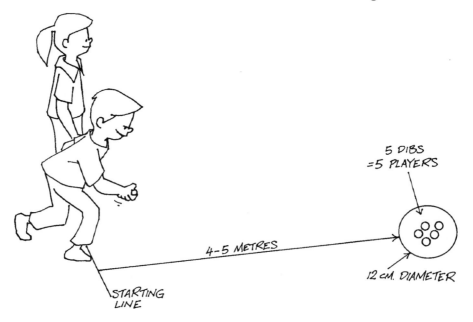

Basic Rules

- Hitting another taw means another shot.
- A taw resting in the ring is a foul shot and the player must repeat the shot on the next turn.
- If a target dib and taw both exit the ring after shooting, this means another shot immediately.
- The taw is fired from its resting place.
- All other marbles must be on the ground while a player is shooting.
- The game continues until all dibs are hit from the ring.
- On the line is 'in'.

Tactics

- Try to get close to the ring to allow an easy shot with the next turn.
- Players can hit their opponents' taws away from the ring with their own taws.
- Always take a shot at a dib if it is as easy as any other offered shot.

Big Ring

Each player places a given number of marbles in a ring of 1 metre in diameter. The starting line is 4–5 metres away.

To determine the order of firing, players throw their marbles from the same place (e.g. the far side of the ring) to see who gets closest to the line.

The aim of the game is to hit the dibs out of the ring.

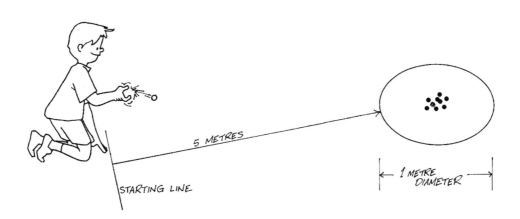

5 METRES

STARTING LINE

1 METRE DIAMETER

Basic rules

- Hitting another taw means another shot.
- A taw resting in the ring is a foul shot and the player must repeat the shot on the next turn.
- If a target dib and taw both exit the ring after shooting, this means another shot immediately.
- The taw is fired from its resting place.
- All other marbles must be on the ground while a player is shooting.
- The game continues until all dibs are hit from the ring.
- On the line is 'in'.

Tactics

- Try to get close to the ring before firing at a dib.
- Fire just hard enough to remove a dib and for the taw to just clear the circle.
- Fire at a cluster rather than a single marble.

Ringer

This is a game for two people only.

Thirteen marbles are placed in a cross formation inside a ring 3 metres in diameter. The starting line is 5 metres from the circle.

In any order, the players fire from the starting line towards the ring. The closest 'lag' gets to fire first at the target marbles.

The winner is to the first to hit seven dibs out of the ring.

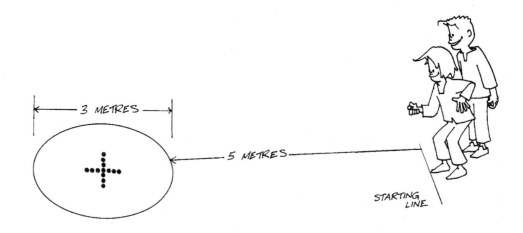

Basic rules

- Each player has their first shot from the edge of the ring.
- For a dib which has been hit out of the ring to be a 'counter', the shooting marble or taw must remain in the ring.
- As long as the taw stays inside the ring the player can continue to fire at the dibs.
- When a shot fails to clear a dib from the ring or the taw itself exits the ring, the other player commences their turn.
- On the line is in.

Double Ring

Two rings: one 12 centimetres in diameter inside a big ring 1 metre in diameter.

The starting line is 5 metres from the big ring.

Players fire from the starting line to manoeuvre (lag) close to the outside of the big ring. Closest goes first to fire at the dibs.

The aim is to shoot the taw at the dibs so that a dib exits the big ring.

STARTING LINE

5 METRES

12 CM.

1 METRE DIAMETER

Basic rules
- Each player takes their first shot from the edge of the big ring.
- If a taw remains in the little ring, exits the big ring', or the dib does not exit the big ring, the player forfeits their turn.
- If a taw hits another taw there is no advantage or penalty.
- The game continues until all the dibs are cleared from the big ring.
- On the line is in.

Trackers

The leader is chosen by the toss of a coin. The leader fires their taw in any direction, the second player follows, the third, and so on. The aim of the game is to hit a particular opponent's taw three times before you are hit three times. When a taw is hit three times that player owes their victor a marble or gains one point.

King Holes

This game is like playing golf with marbles.

There are nine holes situated around a set course. From a starting line each player shoots towards the first hole. If a taw hits another marble, the 'firer' is entitled to a further shot. Similarly, when the taw goes into a hole a further free shot follows. The aim of the game is to get your taw into each of the nine holes in turn. When this is achieved, this taw is a king and if when fired hits another taw then the target taw is knocked out of the game. That player then owes the conqueror a marble or is out, or the firer gains a point (whatever the stakes of the game).

Eye Drops

Each player places a dib in a small ring. Starting order is determined by lagging taws to a given line.

From a standing position astride the little ring the player drops their marbles from above waist height to try and contact the dibs. When a taw knocks a dib from the ring the player gets to keep it.

Twenty-one

The side of a shoe box is cut to make the following holes (the smaller the hole, the more points gained):

- One square hole 4 marbles wide.
- Two triangular holes 2½ marbles wide at the base.
- Two semi-circular holes 1½ marbles in diameter.

 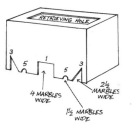

The starting/firing line is 3 metres from the box.

Players lag to the line to determine firing order.

From behind the line each player fires to get their taw through a hole to gain points. The first to 21+ is the winner.

RUNNING AND CHASING GAMES

RUNNING GAMES or 'chasey' are perhaps the purest games of all. Children enjoy the freedom of moving fast over the ground, with the wind in their hair. Chasey is a contest of both body and mind. This chapter contains descriptions of running and chasing games that can involve from 2–30 players.

'It'

'It' (the chaser) can be chosen in many ways. Some methods commonly used are:

* taking turns
* by lot
* by drawing straws
* by guessing numbers
* elimination rhymes
  (e.g. *One potato, two potato, three potato, four;*
  Five potato, six potato, seven potato, more.)

Hide and Seek

'It' choses a home base. This can be a spot on the ground, a post or other object, and acts as 'safe ground' for the other players.

'It' covers their eyes and counts to 100. This gives time for the other players to hide themselves within a specified area.

After this counting/hiding time, 'it' moves around the area trying to locate the hidden players. Once they are seen 'it' runs back to home base and calls 'One, Two, Three!' followed by the players' names and where they were hiding. If this is done before the player can tag home base, then the player concerned is 'out' for the rest of the game. If a player tags home base before being seen or 'called' by 'it' then they are safe for the rest of the game.

Simple Tag (Chasey)

'It' chases the other players until they tag one of them. The tagged player then becomes 'it' and has to chase the others. Usually the second 'it' is not permitted to 'tag back' the first 'it' who tagged them. The game ends by mutual consent or by a player calling 'barley!' (time out).

Team Tag

The group is divided into two teams. One team chases the other, attempting to tag all members of the opposing team within a given time. When tagged, a player must stand still with their arms outstretched. At the end of the time periods, the numbers of 'frees' still running are counted in order to declare the winning team.

Scarecrow Tag

One team chases the other attempting to tag them. When tagged, a player must stand still with legs astride and arms outstretched (a scarecrow). A fellow team member can free a scarecrow by crawling between their legs. A team's turn at being 'it' ends when all members of the other team have been turned into scarecrows. The tagging team that takes the lesser time to capture all scarecrows are the winners.

Hospital Tag

If a player is tagged they become 'it' and must hold the part of the body on which they have been touched. The aim is to touch the opponent's leg below the knee.

Join Up Tag

When 'it' tags a player they must join hands and continue the chase. They can only tag another player while they are joined. When a third player is tagged, they join the line – and so on. The winner is the last 'free' player.

Horses and Jockeys

The 'horses' are free in a paddock. The 'jockeys' run, each to catch their own horses and return to the stable with them. The last horse 'free' wins the game.

Couple Tag

The 'its' chase in couples holding hands. When either is successful in tagging another player, they become 'free', and the player who is touched becomes one of the chasing couple.

All-in Tag

'It' wears a coloured band and tries to tag as many as they can. When tagged the player puts on a band and assists in the tagging. The winner is the last person still running 'free'.

Freeze Tag

A given number of players are 'it'. Chased players when tagged have to stay immobile in exactly the position they held when tagged. A 'free' player may release a 'freeze' by touching them on the hand. The winner is the last 'free' player.

Circle Tag

Players stand around a large marked circle equidistant from each other. On signal they run around the outside of the circle, trying to tag the player immediately in front of them. When a player is tagged they immediately fall out. On a whistle or other signal, the players turn and chase in the opposite direction. The aim is to tag as many others as possible without being tagged themselves.

Two Dogs and a Bone

Players are divided into two teams, numbered off, and positioned on parallel lines approximately 20 metres apart. A beanbag (bone) is placed midway between the two lines.

The leader calls out a number. The respective players from each team run forward and try to collect the bone and return to their place without being tagged by their opponent. Usually both players arrive at the 'bone' at about the same time; so that tactics are to feint and draw, before snatching up the bone and darting back to their line.

Home Base Tag

A marked area is home base. This is a safe area for 'free' players. However, they may stay in home base only for one minute or as long as it takes 'it' to count to 60. Then the free player has to leave the safety of home base immediately.

Torch Tag

This game is played at night with a torch. 'It' has a torch and when the beam is flashed onto a player, 'it' calls out their name. They are then considered tagged and are 'out' for the rest of the game.

Ghost Tag

This game is played at night. All players except 'it' gather in a designated 'home' area and count to 100 while 'it' hides. Players then scatter and try to find the ghost. The ghost ('it') tries to tag the other players before they can make it back to home base. Any players tagged become ghosts during the next round and help the initial 'it'.

Crusts and Crumbs

Players are divided into two teams 'Crusts' and 'Crumbs', seated 1 metre apart. The leader (rolling their Rs to keep suspense) calls out one of the team names. If 'Crusts' is called all players of that team have to get up and run across their safety line (10 metres behind) without being tagged by their corresponding Crumb.

Brandy

This is tag with a ball. 'It' tries to throw the ball to hit a free player below the waist. If a player is hit below the waist by the ball (branded) then they become 'it'.

BALL GAMES

BALL GAMES are probably the most popular games of all. Passed down from generation to generation, many of these games have changed names throughout the years. The games included here require minimal equipment (usually only a ball). They have few and simple rules, and are self-operative. Some games can be played by one lone individual; all can be played by a group. More than other games in this book, ball games can bring about the traits of teamwork, mixing with other children, and the gaining of physical skills.

All of these games are:

- designed to be played in a small area;
- need only one ball;
- can be played by up to 12 players.

Rebound Ball

There are two ways of playing this game:

- Bounce the ball into the ground so that it rebounds back to the next player 'on the full'.
- Throw the ball against the wall so that it bounces once before being gathered by the next player.

The first player (number 1) throws the ball towards the wall and moves quickly to the end of the line. Number 2 moves up to gather the ball, and so on.

   The game can be made competitive by:

- counting the number of successive passes;
- gaining a point for each successful throw and successful catch;
- a player going 'out' if either their throw or catch is unsuccessful.

Rebound Splits

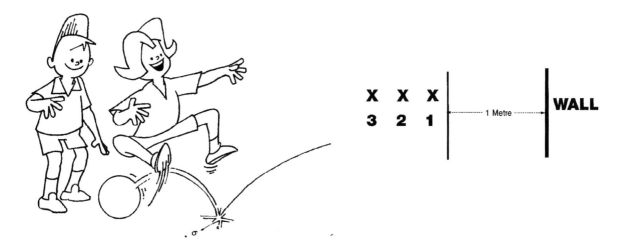

Each player throws the ball against the wall and has to straddle the first bounce on the rebound. Starting 1 metre from the wall, each successful 'throw and straddle' allows the player to move one step back for their next turn. Players learn to vary the height and power of their throw to position the 'bounce point'.

Downball

This game is sometimes called 'handball'. It involves hitting the ball into the ground before it contacts the wall.

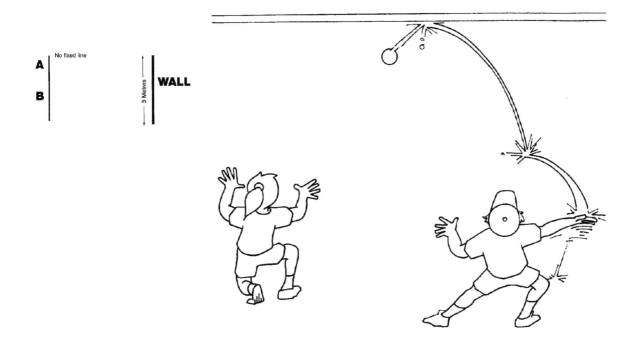

Player A starts the game by bouncing the ball and then hitting it into the ground so that it bounces from the ground to the wall then rebounds. Player B lets the rebound bounce once then hits the ball into the ground to bounce onto the wall, and so on.

- A point is won when the opponent cannot continue the sequence.
- The scoring is as for table tennis: the first to 21 points – advantage.
- Each player has five serves in succession.
- The playing area of the wall is 3 metres wide.

Hoop Ball

Use either a hoop or a circle 1 metre in diameter as the playing area.

This game is handball into a hoop.

Player A starts the serving by bouncing the ball outside the circle then hitting it into the circle. The serve must be relatively gentle as a point cannot be won on the serve alone.

Player B has to return the ball immediately it bounces from the circle, by again hitting it into the circle (this can win a point). The rally continues until the sequence is broken.

- A point is won when a player cannot continue the sequence (except on the return of serve).
- The scoring is as for table tennis: the first to 21 points – advantage.
- Each player has five serves in succession.
- If the ball touches the hoop – it is 'out'.
- Only open-handed hits are allowed.

Four Square (King Ball)

The aim of this game is to get to square 4 and be server/king.

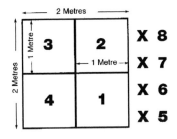

One player stands in each square numbered 1–4. Player 4 (king) stands outside square 4, drops the ball inside their square, then serves the ball underarm into another square. The player that occupies the square in which the ball lands has to hit it into another square. Failure to do so means the player is 'out' and goes to the end of the line. Players inside the squares move anti-clockwise around the squares to replace the outed player. A new player (number 5) comes into the game and always starts in square 1.

* 'On the line' on the outside is 'in'.
* 'On the line' between squares is 'replay'.
* A player is 'out' if they touch the ball before it bounces in their square.
* The ball must be played with open hands.

Dodge Ball in Threes

Players arrange themselves in line. The outside players try to throw the ball to hit the middle player below the waist. This target player jumps and dodges the ball to avoid being hit. When hit the middle person (C) replaces one of the end players (A or B).

Circle Dodge Ball

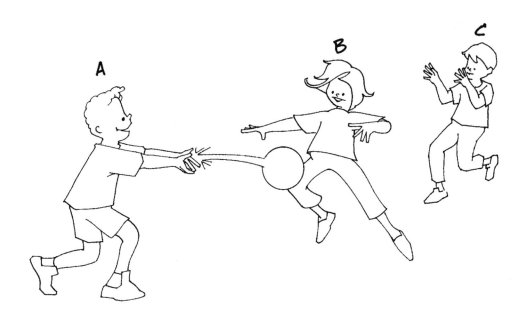

```
A     C     B
X     +     X
```

Four players remain on the outside of the circle and the other players scatter within it. The object of the game is to put out the players inside the circle by hitting them below the waist with the ball, which is thrown by the players outside the circle. The players inside the circle dodge, jump and run about freely to evade the ball. Players who are hit move to the outside of the circle and help with the throwing. The game continues until there is one player left, who is the winner. To speed the game up, two balls can be used.

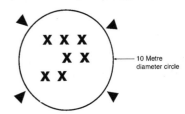

10 Metre diameter circle

Poison Ball

Two players act as throwers at each end of the playing area, while the other players scatter within it. The outside two try to hit the inside players to put them out. If a ball is caught by an inside player 'on the full', that is a 'bag' (life) for them, meaning they can get hit yet not be out for however many 'bags' they have.

When 'out', a player has to sit out of the game, but can be called in by an inside player who can use one of their 'bags' for the purpose. The game continues until there is one player left, who is the winner. The last two players left become the 'enders' for the next round of the game.

Tower Ball

A 'tower' (tin, box or wicket) is placed in the centre of a circle formed by the players. One player is in the centre to defend the tower. The outside players pass the ball around to try and catch the guard on the wrong side of the 'tower' affording them an easy target. The outside player who successfully throws the ball to hit the tower, replaces the centre defender.

Force Back

In pairs equidistant from a centre line, Player A throws the ball towards Player B, throwing for distance. Player B returns the ball from the spot where the ball is caught or lands on the ground. Each player tries to force their opponent back until they are able to catch the return on the opponent's side of the centre line.

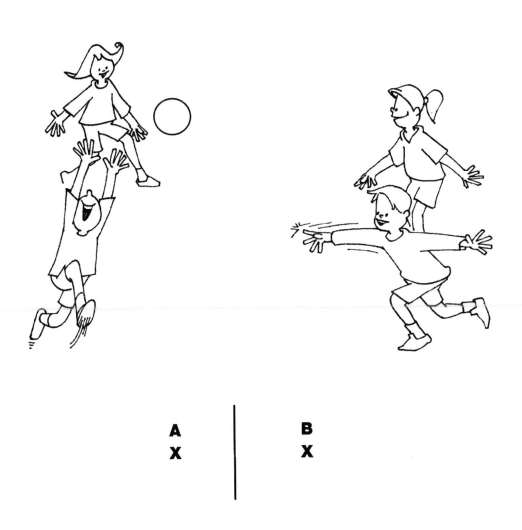

A
X

B
X

Progression Ball

The leader throws the ball to any player who fields or catches the ball and returns it to the leader. A player taking three catches becomes the new leader. A misfield negates a catch.

X

X   X

X   X

X   X

X Leader

100 Up

Targets are painted on a wall displaying scores. Each player has an equal number of shots at the targets – throwing alternately. First to score *exactly* 100 is the winner.

French Cricket

In free spacing, players endeavour to throw the ball (underarm) to strike the 'batter' on the legs (below the knee).

The player who strikes the batter's legs below knee height or who catches the ball on the full after it has been hit becomes the next batter.

Rules can be adjusted, e.g. the batter cannot move the position of their feet; or the batter can move after they strike the ball until the fielder picks it up.

Circle French Cricket

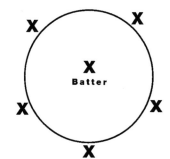

For groups of four to seven players.

Fielders stand around the outside of a circle with the batter in the middle. Fielders use underarm throws and attempt to hit the batter below the knees from outside the circle.

Tether Ball

A game for two players.

A tennis ball is tethered to a string, which in turn is attached to the top of a 3-metre pole.

The two players start on opposite sides of the pole. The server hits the ball with their bat so that the string winds around the pole. The receiver attempts to hit the ball in the opposite direction. Players can hit the ball whenever it is within reach.

The game continues with the players hitting in opposite directions until the ball is 'wound onto' the pole, thereby deciding the winner.

Target Tennis

Target tennis can be played with just a ball, or with a ball and racquets. Using an underarm serve, the player hits the ball (serves) into their opponent's target area. From here, after only one bounce, the ball is played back into the server's area – and so on.

When an error is made, that player leaves the court and is replaced by a waiting player.

This game can be made competitive by:

- A player scoring a point each time their opponent makes a mistake.
- Two or more opposing teams using the same number of opposite squares.

Corner Spry

Each player receives the ball from, and returns it to, the leader; except the last person in line who runs with the ball to the leader's place. The other players move along one place, with the leader moving to the number 1 position.

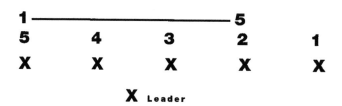

Pig in the Middle

Two outside players pass the ball to each other trying to keep it away from the centre player. When the centre player touches the ball, they replace the player who last threw the ball.

Circle Pass

Players stand in a circle, numbered off. The centre person (number 1) passes the ball to number 2 and then runs to take the place of number 2. Number 2 runs into the centre and passes to number 3, then runs to take the place of number 3, and so on.

Wandering Ball

Players in a circle number off. Then number 1 goes into the centre. The outside players pass the ball to each other while the centre player (number 1) tries to touch the ball. Players cannot move their feet when they have the ball. When number 1 touches the ball, number 2 enters the circle and takes over the contest, and so on.

Keepings Off

For two teams of two to six players.

Each team tries to keep the ball away from the other. The ball must be passed by throwing. Players cannot run when they have the ball.

Donkey

All players stand in a loosely formed circle. The starting thrower hurls the ball high into the air and calls another player's name as they do so. Everyone scatters as fast as they can, except the player whose name has been called.

If this 'named player' catches the ball before it lands, they can immediately toss again, and call a different player's name.

As soon as they obtain the ball, whether by a catch or gather, the named player yells 'freeze'! All other players must stop immediately and freeze their position. The named player then calls the name of another who is the target, e.g. 'Helene'. This name has six letters, which entitles the player with the ball to take six steps towards the target player (who is still 'frozen'), before throwing the ball at them.

If the throw hits the target player, they get the letter 'D'. If the ball misses or is caught by the target player, the thrower gets the letter 'D'. The game continues to spell the word 'donkey'.

All players then reassemble at the central point again, where the player who gained the last letter restarts the game with a throw. The game continues until one player gets the six letters in 'donkey'. Now the game can either start from the very beginning or that player can simply sit out the rest of the game, until there is a single winner.

Blanket Ball

A blanket is hung across a rope, line or net, so that at its top it is 2 metres high. This makes a screen through which players are unable to see their opponents. Many games can be played over this blanket: from throwing the ball over the net to gain a point if it touches the ground inside a prescribed area, to volleyball or newcombe.

King Ball

Players stand in a circle with their legs astride and feet touching their neighbours' feet. Using a large soft ball such as a volleyball, players try to hit the ball through someone else's legs. Legs must remain straight, hands are not to rest on the ground, and open hands are used to hit the ball. When the ball passes between two players on the way out of the circle this is a 'window' and is a replay. When the ball passes through a player's legs, they gain a point, fetch the ball, and restart the game.

At the end of a given time, e.g. 5 minutes, the player with the least points is the winner or 'King'.

Box Ball

This game is played on a diamond. Play is started by the pitcher underarming the ball across the home plate. The batter uses their open hand or clenched fist to hit the ball so that it lands somewhere within the playing area (the box). If the ball first lands outside the box, the batter is out. This automatically means all fouls are out. In the remainder of the game softball/baseball rules apply.

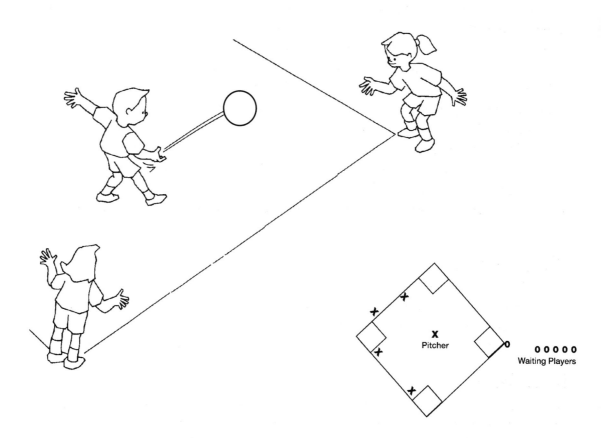

Bin Ball

Players form a circle around an upturned rubbish bin.

Number 1 player is the 'King' and starts the game by throwing a tennis ball against the bin. Other players must field the ball as it rebounds.

If the ball fails to hit the bin when thrown or a player fails to field it cleanly, they go to the end of the line and everyone moves up one space. The aim of the game is to get to number 1 position – 'King'.

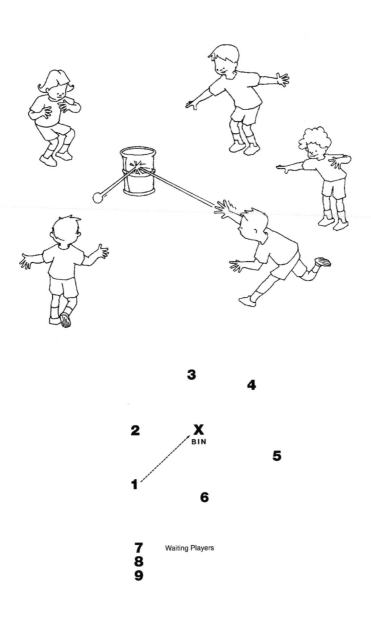

3

4

2   **X**
          BIN

5

1

6

7   Waiting Players
8
9

Shed Ball

As the name implies, this game is played over a shed. The ball is thrown over the barrier where opponents try to catch it on the full. If a catch is unsuccessful the ball is thrown back again and so on, until there is a successful catch. When a catch is made the entire catching team runs either way around the shed and tries to tag their opponents. When the umpire blows their whistle the chasing stops.

Tagged players join the chasing team and restart the game by another throw. The game is over when there is only one player left on one of the teams.

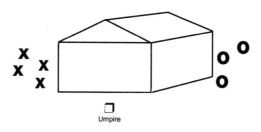

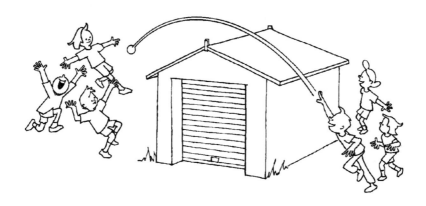

Town Ball

The first player rolls the ball into each square in turn, and must retrieve it before it rolls out. When a mistake is made, the player moves to the end of the line.

When a player has achieved this 'roll and retrieve' into all six areas they may initial the Town Roll in the appropriate column.

Then they tackle the next task, e.g.:

- lob – one bounce – catch
- foot pass – retrieve.

The first player to initial all columns becomes Mayor.

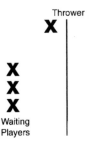

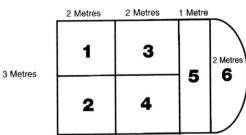

SCORING
GAMES

THESE GAMES are best played by 1–4 people. Any more than this means waiting too long for a 'turn'. If being played by more than four, then extra sets of equipment would be needed, to allow several games to be played simultaneously (for example, six sets for 25 children). Most of these scoring games are best played on a smooth surface. Each game is described, the necessary equipment outlined, and the scoring explained.

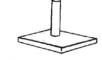

Quoits

Equipment
- Six rope quoits, approximately 15 centimetres in diameter.
- One stake or peg, approximately 2.5 centimetres thick and 30 centimetres high. This may be driven into the ground or be on a stable base plate.

A line is drawn on the ground approximately 3 metres from the stake. The first player tosses their quoits, one at a time, from behind the throwing line. The aim is to get each quoit to fall completely over the stake so that it encircles it (this is termed a 'ringer').

Players take turns to toss all six quoits, one at a time. The throwing technique found most successful is; underarm and overhand, tossing the quoit so that the leading edge passes over the top of the stake but the trailing edge catches the stake, causing the quoit to fall on it.

Decide on a goal (e.g. 25 points). The first player to reach this score in equal turns is the winner. A tied game is decided in a 'sudden death' play off, where the first quoit missed (on equal turns) means elimination.

Horseshoes

Equipment

- 2–6 horseshoes. If horseshoes are unavailable or thought to be inappropriate, rubber deck tennis quoits can be used.
- A stake or peg, approximately 2.5 centimetres thick and 30 centimetres high. This may be driven into the ground or be on a stable base plate.
- The stake is positioned 12–15 metres from the throwing line.

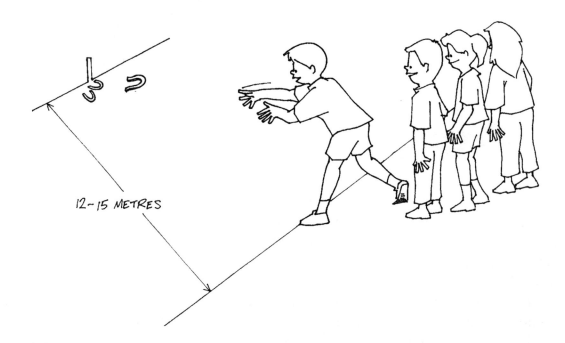

12–15 METRES

The first player tosses their horseshoes, one at a time, to land as near as possible to the stake. The thrower then collects the items they threw, and hands them to the second thrower. Then the second player throws, and the next, etc. All players must remain at the throwing end.

Scoring

Decide on a goal (e.g. 10 points). The first player to this score in equal turns is the winner.

Pairs
- If player 1's closest horseshoe is nearer to the stake than player 2's, player 1 gets one point.
- The closer of the remaining two shoes also gets a point.
- A ringer (horseshoe wrapped around the stake) is worth 3 points.

More than two people
- Players get 2 points for the nearest shoe.
- Players get 1 point for the second nearest shoe.
- A ringer is worth 3 points.
- This game is usually played to 10 points.

Penny Pitching

Equipment
- An equal number of pennies per player (these 'pennies' can be old imperial currency or decimal 20-cent coins).
- Starting line 2–4 metres from the wall.

Taking it in turns, each player tosses their penny from the starting line (2–4 metres from the wall) to get as close as possible to the wall. The player with the penny nearest to the wall is the winner.

Depending on the game decided, the winner of that 'turn' either keeps all the other pennies or gets a point. The player who accumulates the most pennies or is the first to reach a target score is the winner.

A variation is that the penny must hit the wall first before falling to the ground. A penny that does not hit the wall first cannot be the winner.

Deck Tennis (Quoit Tennis)

Equipment

- One rubber or rope quoit.
- A net or a rope across the court 2 metres high.
- Court.

This game may be played by two to four people, as for singles and doubles tennis.

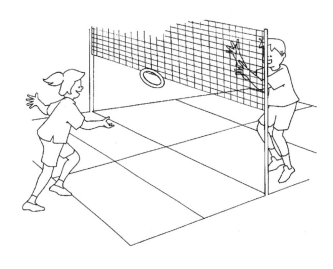

A player serves from behind the back line and the throw must be made by an underarm or horizontal action of the wrist and elbow. The arm must not be raised above the shoulder at any time during the service or throw. The quoit must pass over the net into the service court diagonally opposite. When serving, no lets are allowed. If the quoit touches the net and falls over, the service is taken again.

Scoring

Scoring is the same as for tennis.

Rules

- In catching the quoit, the right or left hand may be used, but not the two together. A clean catch must be made, i.e., no other part of the body may be used to hold the quoit.
- Either hand may be used to throw.
- The return is made from the stance where the quoit is caught.
- A point is lost to the receiver when the quoit is allowed to fall to the ground, and to the thrower when the quoit passes under the rope or falls outside the court.

Frisbee

Equipment

At least one frisbee, but a number (one for each player) is an advantage.

Distance Throw

From behind a line, in turn, each player throws the frisbee as far as they can. Distance is measured from where the frisbee first contacts the ground. Usually the winner is decided from the best of three throws.

Target Throw

From behind a line, in turn, each player throws to hit a nominated target (e.g. a tree). The winner is the first to hit the target from an equal number of throws. If there is an initial tie, a throw off where the closest from one throw each, is declared the winner.

Throw and Catch

Partners stand each behind a designated line. From behind these lines the partners throw the frisbee to each other. The winners are the pair that can make the most consecutive passes without dropping the frisbee.

Stunt Throwing

- 'Boomerang' – a player both throws and catches the frisbee.
- Catching one hand.
- Catching one finger.
- Throwing from under one leg, etc.

Shuffleboard (Disc Quoits)

Equipment
- Three quoits per player.
- Target of three concentric circles.

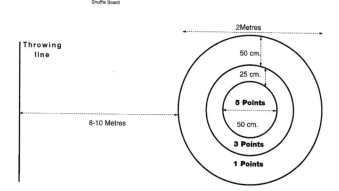

Shuffle Board

Throwing line

2Metres

50 cm.

25 cm.

5 Points

8-10 Metres

50 cm.

3 Points

1 Points

Each player in turn throws three quoits from behind the 'throwing line' to try and land in the target area. A score is totalled from where the quoits lie. If a quoit is lying in two score zones (no matter what percentage), the lower score counts. First to a target score (e.g. 25 points) in an equal amount of turns is the winner. A tie is decided by a single 'throw off'.

Skittles

Equipment

- 10 cones, blocks, tin cans, etc., to act as skittles/targets.
- One tennis ball.

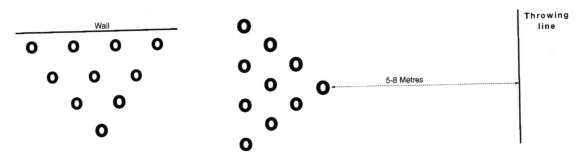

This game is played with a wall as a backstop.

The skittles are arranged in an equilateral triangle so that the ball can just pass between any pair. These positions should be marked on the ground, so the skittles can be easily replaced after being knocked down.

Using an underarm roll or bowl from a 'throwing line' (5–8 metres from the skittles), players take it in turn to try to knock over these skittles.

There are three variations to this game:

- The first player continues to bowl/roll until all 10 skittles have been knocked down. The least number of bowls determines the winner.
- Player one has a single bowl, then counts the number of skittles downed. Player two follows, and so on. The first to a target score (e.g. 25) is the winner.
- Place the skittles close to the wall so that a rebounding ball can also knock down skittles.

Hopscotch Golf

From behind the starting line players try to kick their marker (taw) into space 1. After this initial kick they must hop after their taw and use this hopping foot for all other kicks. Each kick is counted.

When successful at space 1 they return to the starting line to play space 2, and so on. Each turn is begun from the starting line. The player to complete the course in the fewest number of kicks is the winner.

Grand Prix

Equipment
- One free-running miniature car per player, i.e., matchbox, dinky toy, etc.
- A designated course along a paved area (the more circuitous the better).

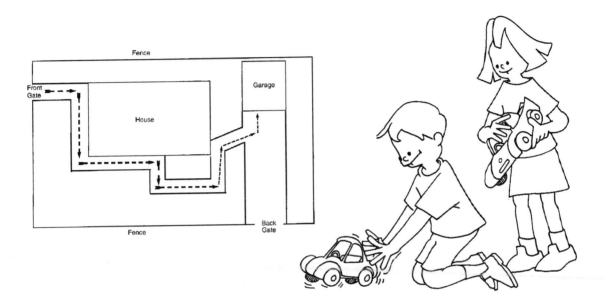

EXAMPLE COURSE:
From the front gate – to the front of the house – along the front – down the side of the house – half way across the back – down through the lawn – along the drive to the garage.

Taking turns, players push and release their cars to travel as far as possible along the desired route. If a car overturns the next push may be retaken from the previous starting point. Each subsequent push is taken from where the car comes to rest.

From an equal amount of turns, the first car to reach the finishing line is the winner.

Mini Golf

Equipment

- One golf putter or implement to use as such.
- One golf or tennis ball per player.
- A designated course along a paved area (the more circuitous the better).

EXAMPLE COURSE:

Along the footpath in front of the house – in the front gate – down the drive – along the path around the front of the house – down the side of the house – along the back of the house – to hit the garage wall.

Taking alternate turns, players putt the ball along the desired route. Each ball must be played from where it comes to rest. From an equal amount of turns the first ball to reach the finish line is the winner.

INDEX OF GAMES